THE SECRETS OF A Savvy Traveler

BY PRISCILLA SMILEY

outskirtspress

DENVER, COLORADO

The Secrets of a Savvy Traveler

Outskirts Press, Inc.
http://www.outskirtspress.com

ISBN: 978-1-4787-3271-6

Outskirts Press and the "OP" logo are trademarks belonging to Outskirts Press, Inc.

PRINTED IN THE UNITED STATES OF AMERICA

Contents

The Secrets of a Savvy Traveler v

Barriers That Keep You from Traveling 1

Why Should You Travel? 4

The 3 Ps of Traveling: Paper, Plastic, and Purchase . 10

The Savvy Traveler 30

Dos and Don'ts 30

Planning: 'Tis the Season 47

Planning: Planes, Trains, and Automobiles 52

Planning: Passports, Visas, and Immunizations 66

The Planning Process: 71

Places to Stay 71

Execution 77

Outcome 81

The Secrets of a Savvy Traveler

I DREAMED OF traveling—horseback riding on the beaches of Turks and Caicos, seeing the lights in Tokyo, and feeling the raw iron of the Eiffel Tower beneath my feet. The problem was that for much of my early life . . . that's all it was . . . a dream.

Have you ever envisioned yourself riding a camel across the Arabian Desert before catching a water taxi to shop at Dubai's gold and spice souk, bungee jumping off the Tower of Macau in Hong Kong before jetting to Cape Town, South Africa, to swim with the great white sharks to satisfy your thirst for danger?

I know you as the reader are just where I was. But I can lead you out of your dreams and give you the tools needed to take you on the experiences of a lifetime. One day I made the first step on my journey to becoming a savvy traveler—capable of finding the best deals to travel as often as I wanted, without borders. It will take some planning, but you can become savvy too.

Reading my book will teach you the possibility of all of your future explorations, from vacationing on an exotic isle while relaxing under the sun and getting a tan to cruising across the Atlantic, Pacific, or Indian oceans while enjoying your view from a multilevel ship. Never again should you only daydream about exploring the world and creating magical moments by traveling to distant lands. Behold, here are the keys that will unlock the Secret to becoming a Savvy Traveler.

Before I became a savvy traveler, I would sit and fantasize for hours or even days about traveling to the seven continents and seas. I would dream about where I would explore, who I would meet, and what I would see on all of my journeys. However, it wasn't until five years ago that I decided to stop dreaming and to start living. I decided that I would not die without seeing this great world God created and reach every continent during the process.

The problem was, I had the desire to travel but did not know where to begin or how I would finance my future journeys. I knew the first thing I had to accomplish was to learn to think outside of the box, which required exiting my comfort zone. Many in my family and circle of friends were content with being born and dying in the city of their birth. They seemed to be just fine without exploring life. Many of them did not have a passport book or a passport card and have never even left the state of Florida. I knew there was so much more to life, and I knew I wanted much more.

At the age of twenty-five, I applied for my first

passport book and within five short years, the world had been my oyster. I have been blessed to travel to Asia, Africa, the Middle East, Europe, Mexico, and the Caribbean. I explored the seas by way of cruises and yachts, safaried the bushes of Africa on the backs of elephants while chasing lions and leopards in an open Jeep Wrangler and backpacked throughout Europe while visiting different cities and touring historical sites. I soaked up sun and played in the sands on the islands of Grand Cayman, Jamaica, and Puerto Rico, while parasailing off the coast of the Bahamas and zip lining through the jungles of Mexico. I vacationed in all of these places and created countless memories because I was determined to travel. Traveling became my passion. I wanted to travel. I needed to travel. My goal was to tour the world, and I was determined to allow nothing or no one to hinder me from accomplishing my goal.

Since obtaining my passport book, I set a goal for myself to explore every continent during the next seven years. This goal would require me to take a minimum of one international trip per year. Setting this goal created a challenge for me. I would not only have a lot of traveling to complete, but I would also have to be able to finance my trips. Growing up in a single-parent household where finances were limited, my mother taught me the importance of saving money. As I got older, I realized how the lack of finances could place limitations on a person's life, and I was determined to never allow finances to hinder me from accomplishing any of my goals, especially my new goal of traveling.

Through research and experience, I've learned that traveling can be affordable on almost anyone's budget. I was inspired to write this book to encourage and demonstrate how to turn traveling dreams into reality. Throughout my traveling journeys, I have learned from my experiences and created a list of ways to travel economically, a list of dos and don'ts of traveling, and how to budget and pay for traveling. Follow me throughout my journey as you learn the foundation of how to create your own traveling memories.

CHAPTER 1

Barriers That Keep You from Traveling

PEOPLE COME UP with various reasons why seeing the world, venturing off to fun and exciting places, or just taking a break from the normal hustle and bustle is not an option. These people allow many misconceptions to hinder them from traveling. Some feel it's too expensive, or it's almost impossible to get that amount of time off from work, while others feel they need a traveling companion. Allowing these misconceptions to influence your decision to travel can prevent you from seeing what the world has to offer. So allow me to show you how to overcome these misconceptions.

Misconception #1. Traveling is too expensive.

In life we spend money on things we want. Whether it is a designer handbag, a luxury car, golf clubs, or season tickets . . .If we want it, we will find the means to pay for it. Traveling should be the same way.

Traveling the world is actually very affordable as long as you do it right. The three main necessities for traveling are: transportation to get you to where you're going, accommodations to relax and stay at while you are there, and food to eat. If you are realistic in your expectations of where you would like to visit and create a budget, you could add a stamp to your passport for less than a monthly car note payment.

Misconception #2. It's impossible to get that amount of time off of work.

Many of us work eight hours a day, five days a week. Whenever I planned a trip, I would ask my employer if I could work a compressed workweek. This allowed me to work ten hours a day, four days a week. Working a compressed workweek gave me an extra day off by allowing me to enjoy a three-day weekend—Thus, a savings of a vacation day.

Working a compressed workweek not only benefited me, it also benefited my employer. I was able to complete all of my assigned duties for that workweek, and I did not have to leave anything incomplete until I returned.

Combining your company paid holidays with your vacation days can also help you save on the amount of vacation time you use. Taking trips around Labor Day or Thanksgiving will give you those *extra* days off, allowing you to use less of your vacation or personal time.

Misconception #3. I need a traveling companion.

As the world evolves, this has become less and less true. There are many types of traveling groups designed for individuals who want to travel but feel as if they have no one to go with. These traveling groups cater to everyone's needs, from women-only traveling groups to people who want to solo travel. These groups are advertised on the Internet, and if interested, all you have to do is contact them and obtain information. Easy as 1-2-3!

Now, if you're that individual who is not interested in traveling with people you do not know, I would recommend you sell the idea of traveling to family and friends. My experience has shown me that, in general, people want to travel. They just don't know how. Selling the idea of traveling or why everyone should travel can help you do just that.

CHAPTER 2

Why Should You Travel?

PEOPLE OFTEN ASK me about my love for traveling and my desire to do so. They often ask me why I travel as frequently as I do and what satisfaction does traveling bring. Traveling provides me with a strong sense of independence. It allows me the freedom to do whatever I want, whenever I want, and as often as I want. I am the designer of my voyages. I determine where I will go, when I should go, and how I will get there. Even when surprises come up I get the satisfaction of making an adventure out of them and deciding my next step.

Traveling will change your life. This chapter will explain why you and everyone should travel. So, if you ever wondered what is the point of traveling or what you can gain from traveling, allow me to describe what I believe are some of its major benefits.

1. Traveling=Relaxation. Relaxation is my means of unwinding from my everyday demand such as work, family, and bills, and gives me a break from the routine. Whether at a beach, a park, or enjoying scenery from my daily drive, relaxation is a good way to relieve stress and enjoy life.

2. Traveling=Freedom for self-expression and exploration. Traveling allows me to be free to self-express and explore all the qualities that make me unique. My definition of self-expression is not being afraid of being oneself. In our everyday lives we have many roles defined by family, work, and our community. However, while traveling or on vacation, you don't have to play these roles. You can just be yourself and enjoy quality time with you and thus, re-discover the true you.

3. Traveling=Sightseeing. Let's face it, there is so much out there to see. From the natural wonders of the world to each country's main tourist attractions, traveling allows you to witness the beauty of them all. When I was in Dubai, I had the opportunity to visit two of their famous tourist attractions: the world's only man-made islands, the Palm Islands, which are in the shape of a palm tree, and the world's tallest man-made building—the Burj Khalifa,

which is a skyscraper in the heart of downtown Dubai.

While in South Africa, I visited Table Mountain which forms part of the Table Mountain National Park. To get to the top, visitors can either hike or ascend by Cableway car and view Cape Town from over three thousand five hundred feet above sea level. These landmarks not only offered historical facts but also epic views of the cities, and trust me when I tell you, witnessing these views in person is absolutely remarkable.

4. Traveling=Gaining an appreciation for different cultures and beliefs. I enjoy learning about different cultures and ways of life. Dubai taught me the differences between the American and the Middle Eastern culture and traditions. I was surprised to realize that many of our values were universal while our traditions were not. The emphasis placed on the value of hospitality in both cultures was the same, while the difference in traditional clothing attire amongst men and women was not.

5. Traveling=Learning new languages and meeting new people. When traveling to different countries, one is able to learn new languages and meet new people. This allows you to be

more open-minded and gain a better perspective on how others live outside of your native home.

6. Traveling=Savoring new foods. Since I am a foodie, traveling allows me to be adventurous and experience foods I would have never had the opportunity to taste in my native country. I never thought I would have sampled "game meats," such as crocodile, impala, or zebra, until I vacationed in South Africa or tasted turtle soup until I traveled to the island of Grand Cayman.

   If interested in sampling authentic dishes on a budget, many countries offer food tours and cooking classes as independent excursions. Food tours can include eating in the privacy of a local's home, local specialty stores, or old mom-and-pop eateries and food stalls which are similar to a food truck in the U.S. These tours are normally walking tours and may include the sampling of authentic drinks as well as teas.

7. Traveling=Creating everlasting memories. Traveling allows you to create memories of all your first-time experiences. Memories of the first time you hiked a mountain or skied the slopes. These are something you

will never forget, and besides photos, a physical reminder or keepsake is a great way to always remember your traveling adventure.

I believe every savvy traveler should have a souvenir collection. Souvenir collections come in all forms, including postcards, stamps, shot glasses, china, mugs, and magazines. Each collection depends upon the interests of the individual person.

When I began my souvenir collection, I chose shot glasses because I wanted something small in size that could be easily toted. Today, I have over fifty shot glasses in my collection. I store my shot glasses in a glass window in my home as a wonderful reminder of the many memories from each destination I have traveled. These constant reminders also let me know me that I have so much more traveling ahead.

8. Traveling=Eliminating Regrets. People may often want to travel but have many reasons why they cannot. Some may wish to obtain a college or graduate degree, start a family, or secure steady employment before they tour the world. Oftentimes once that college or graduate degree is completed or steady employment

is secured, they tend to find another reason as to why they should wait to travel.

The majority of the people I know who procrastinated traveling never did. Later in life they had regrets and wished they would have taken advantage of previous traveling opportunities. I believe people procrastinate out of fear of getting out of their comfort zone or feeling that traveling is beyond their reach. Once you can envision yourself doing anything, then those visions can become reality as long as you believe and create a plan. Yes, traveling does cost money; however, you most definitely do not need to be wealthy to do so.

9. Traveling=Experiencing an adrenaline rush. Research has shown me that when on vacation travelers become more adventurous and are open to trying new things. From hang gliding in Brazil to paragliding in France, trying something different and exhilarating is welcomed by savvy travelers. Maybe it's the bragging rights after the adrenaline rush is what these travelers love.

10. Traveling=Having FUN!!!! While on vacation, you should do whatever excites and allows you to have fun. Simple as that.

CHAPTER **3**

The 3 Ps of Traveling: Paper, Plastic, and Purchase

THERE'S NO NEED to break the bank. Traveling can be inexpensive and in some cases downright cheap! Over the years I have learned research will show you how to locate the best deal possible while being flexible with your travel dates and times, which will reduce the cost of your trip by hundreds, if not thousands, of dollars.

Below are my Travel $avers, better known as the 3 Ps of Traveling. These tips will help you keep costs down and are broken down into three categories: paper, plastic, and purchase.

1. Paper. No obligation required.

- Take advantage and sign up for frequent flyer accounts with different airline companies. Frequent flyer accounts are absolutely

FREE! This is something like a "Thank You" that the airline companies offer to their customers for being loyal.

Airline companies allow their customers the opportunity to earn frequent flyer miles that can be redeemed for airline tickets, travel and transportation, shopping and dining, donations to charities, and excursions. Some even have online auctions where members can partake and have a chance to win a variety of items like basketball, baseball, and football tickets. Frequent flyer miles can also be used to upgrade your flight seat from economy class to economy comfort or first/business class.

The main thing I love about a frequent flyer miles account is that it acts just like a rewards card, which you will soon learn about. You are not only able to earn miles with flights taken with your frequent flyer airline carriers; you can also earn miles with companies that are affiliated with the carrier. For example, Delta Airlines is affiliated with different companies from rental car companies to restaurants. Every time a purchase is made using your frequent flyer number, you will have the opportunity to earn miles that can be redeemed for future use.

Now, in order to earn these miles, you will have to register a credit card to your frequent flyer account. I would recommend signing up for a frequent flyer account with every airline carrier you fly. This way, every time you purchase an airline ticket and take a flight, you are earning miles toward future redemption. Some things to look for when signing up for frequent flyer accounts are blackout dates, expiration dates of miles, rollover miles, and whether there is a cap on the amount of miles members can earn annually.

• Hotel companies offer rewards programs too. Many hotel groups allow you to sign up and earn rewards that can be redeemed for free night stays, travel and transportation, shopping, dining, and donation to charities. Every night stayed at a hotel group or its partner hotels puts you one step closer to redeeming points for future usage. Many hotel chains offer an honor or preferred guest program free of charge for all its members.

Anyone is able to sign up and can begin earning honor or preferred guest points immediately. Essentially, the amount of points earned depends upon the amount of nights stayed and the amount of money spent on the hotel room. Each honor or preferred guest program offers different membership tiers with bonus rewards from late checkout to extra night stays.

2. Plastic. Reward yourself. Apply for the best credit or check card that offers travel rewards.

- One way to save money is to apply for a credit card or check cards that offer rewards points. These cards are typically known as rewards cards. Banks and credit card companies offer a variety of rewards cards that their members can use to earn rewards points. Points are earned by making purchases on these cards. These rewards points can later be redeemed or used for traveling and other rewards bonuses like free or reduced airline tickets, hotel stays, merchandise, and/or excursions.

- Many credit card companies and banks allow their members to earn one point per dollar spent and usually every ten thousand points earned can be redeemed for one hundred dollars or every one thousand points can be redeemed for ten dollars. Luckily, you don't have to spend ten thousand dollars to get ten thousand points. There's a cheaper and easier way. Many credit card companies and banks offer double and/or even triple rewards points for everyday purchases, such as gas, drugs, and grocery store purchases. Receiving more points on single purchases will allow you to earn points more rapidly to redeem for future purchases.

• Another thing to consider when choosing a credit card or check card is to find out if it offers rewards points for miles flown. Miles flown is the flight distance between the point of origin and your final destination. This is very important because you earn points at a faster rate, especially if you get a rewards card, which offers the maximum traveling benefit. For example, my Citibank rewards credit card offers one rewards point for every mile flown by me and each additional airline ticket purchased for family and friends I make on my credit card. If I purchase an airline ticket for myself and three of my friends, I earn points on miles flown for all four all airline tickets. You could earn enough points on one trip to cover your next flight.

• You can also redeem those points for excursions, electronics, and gift cards, or anything your credit card company offers. I can remember when I wanted to take a helicopter tour of the Grand Canyon in Grand Canyon, Arizona. The tour itself was about three hundred and fifty dollars per person, a total of seven hundred dollars for two. It included a scenic view of Nevada and Arizona and an intimate champagne lunch in the heart of the Grand Canyon. I could not imagine the idea of paying seven hundred dollars for any excursion. So I decided to redeem my "Thank-You" rewards points I earned on my rewards credit card, and I was able to purchase my excursions at a discounted rate of two hundred fifty dollars for two helicopter tickets, which was a savings of four hundred and fifty dollars.

• Several credit and check cards offer rewards points for specific hotel chains and airline carriers. For example, American Airlines may have an agreement with Citibank Credit Card and Hilton Hotels may have an agreement with an American Express Credit Card. These cards allow you to redeem points for tickets with their partner airline companies as well as free hotel nights.

It is important for you to determine if you would like a card that is affiliated with a particular airline carrier and its partner hotels as you will not be able to earn or redeem points for nonaffiliated airlines or hotels. That's why when choosing a credit card or check card that is airline specific, research their partner airline companies to see your options for flying with their carriers to potentially earn rewards points for future redemption.

- Look for a rewards credit card that offers annual companion airline tickets. A companion airline ticket is a discounted or free ticket given to the person who accompanies the rewards credit card holder on a trip. These companion tickets can be redeemed when the credit card holder purchases a qualifying plane ticket, and with some credit card companies, the qualifying plane ticket has to be over a certain amount.

  The companion ticket can be used by anyone of your choice and can be refundable and may not have blackout dates. Having a credit card that offers this perk is a great way for you to save money toward your travels since many times airfare can be the greatest expense when planning a trip.

- Many credit cards that offer rewards points have an annual fee. Annual fees can be pricey depending on the credit card, and many companies may waive the annual fee for the first year you are a new credit card holder. Research the credit cards that do not offer annual fees and research the benefits of those credit cards.

The first rewards credit card I applied for did not have an annual fee. I was interested in a credit card that would offer me rewards for miles flown on airlines that I could later redeem for reduced or free flights. One of the benefits of the credit card I chose was just that; it included earning one rewards point for every three miles flown for myself and all other airline tickets purchased on my credit card.

There was another credit card I could have applied for that had an annual fee of seventy-five dollars. That credit card offered one rewards point for every mile flown for myself and all other airline tickets purchased on my rewards card as well. Initially, I thought earning one rewards point for every three flown was a really good deal. I thought why pay the seventy-five-dollar annual fee when I could earn rewards points for free.

It wasn't until I decided to fly to Europe when I realized that having the credit card with the annual fee offered me the better benefits and would help me in attaining my goal for reduced or free flights at a faster rate. The total miles flown for my flight to Europe was twelve thousand miles. With the credit card without the annual fee, I received four thousand rewards points, one point for every three miles flown. But if I had the credit card that offered the better benefits, the one with the annual fee, I would have received twelve thousand rewards points.

I realized that I cheated myself out of eight thousand rewards points by not having the right credit card that offered me the best value for what I wanted. In my opinion, the benefits gained from credit cards that have rewards programs but also have an annual fee outweigh the cost of their annual fee. My recommendation is for you to make sure the credit card for which you are paying the annual fee offers everything you need and want to obtain your goal of having that rewards card.

3. Purchase. Ready, Set, Go! Knowing how to combine deals and when to get flights and hotels will save you a bundle.

    • Now that I've shared the value of having frequent flyer accounts and credit or debit card accounts that offer rewards points, the next step is to illustrate how combining rewards from both can offer you the best benefit.

    When I purchased both of my airplane tickets to Dubai and Japan, I used my rewards points earned from my credit card. At the time, the going rate for a plane ticket to

Dubai was starting at one hundred twenty thousand rewards points or one thousand two hundred fifty-nine dollars, depending on flight time, departure date, stops, and airline companies. However, I only had about thirty thousand rewards points. So I decided to redeem my thirty thousand points and reduce the price of my airline fare. My ticket went from one thousand two hundred fifty-nine dollars to nine hundred fifty-nine dollars, a savings of three hundred dollars. Since I purchased my ticket with an airline company in which I was a frequent flyer member, I was able to earn miles for mileage flown on my Dubai trip even though I purchased my ticket for a discounted fare by redeeming my rewards points earned with my rewards credit card.

Once I saw how easy it was to earn and redeem benefits at the same time, I repeated this process again when I decided to travel to Japan. This time, I had over sixty thousand rewards points that I was able to redeem with my rewards credit card. My airfare to Japan was starting at nine hundred dollars. Once I redeemed my rewards points, my airfare price reduced from nine hundred dollars to seventy-one dollars and nine cents, round-trip, a savings of over eight hundred dollars.

My friends and family could not believe I purchased my airfare to Japan for less than one hundred dollars.

Again, I chose an airline company in which I was a frequent flyer member and earned over twenty thousand miles, almost enough miles to redeem for a free airline ticket with my frequent flyer account carrier. Over the years, I have repeated this process numerous times, and I have been able to fly to Atlanta, Denver, Los Angeles, New York, and Toronto, Canada, all free of charge. You can't beat that!

• Unfortunately, the same does not work vice versa. Many frequent flyer accounts do not allow you to redeem miles to reduce the cost of an airline ticket. You must have all the requested miles or be willing to purchase the missing miles before you can purchase your ticket. In addition, there are added fees such as taxes you will have to pay even after redeeming your frequent flyer miles and before purchasing your plane ticket.

Once miles have been redeemed, you will not be able to earn points for miles flown with your frequent flyer accounts. For instance, you redeemed your miles and purchased an airline ticket. Because you redeemed your frequent flyer miles, you will not be able to earn additional miles for miles flown. You will also not be able to earn rewards points on your credit card because you did not purchase your plane ticket with that credit card. Thus, when using frequent flyer miles to purchase airfare, there is no way to earn multiple points or combine points for future usage. However, do not let this discourage you. As we previously learned, these ac-counts are FREE. So anytime you are able to receive something FREE of charge, be sure to take advantage of it.

• Purchase airline tickets in advance, prefer-ably in the beginning of the week. My re-search has shown me that airline ticket prices increase around midweek. Booking early-morning or late-night flights can also save money. These flights tend to be the least desired, which is great for the pockets of a savvy traveler. For my friend's twenty-fifth birthday, we decided to head to Puerto Rico. To obtain the best deal, we had to de-part on a Wednesday morning at seven a.m. The money we saved by choosing to take the early-morning flight allowed us to have extra spending money while on our trip.

Please note that just because you don't pur-chase during these times, it does not mean you will not be able to get a less-expensive fare price. However, from my experience, you are more likely to get a better price if you are willing to fly at the times previously mentioned. Also, purchasing plane tickets months in advance can also save you money. Waiting less than twenty-one days before your desired flight date to purchase your ticket can cost a pretty penny. Always remember that time is of the essence to lock in a good rate, so be savvy and book in advance.

• Traveling midweek as compared to weekends can also save money. Research shows traveling on weekends is more expensive because of high demand. More travelers choose to travel on weekends for convenience, whether for work or pleasure. Since weekends are high in demand and there is a limited supply of seats on airplanes, airlines are able to increase prices, and thereby, increase their profitability. However, during midweek, many of the airline companies offer discounted tickets because the demand for seats is lower. This allows savvy travelers to save money, and always remember, money saved on booking a trip can be used as spending money while on the trip.

• Hotel rooms tend to work the same way as

airline tickets. Hotels are usually more affordable during the week as compared to weekends because of supply and demand. Traveling weekdays can save money and allow you to have increased access to hotel amenities since the hotel may be less crowded during the week as compared to weekends.

- Avoid traveling during peak seasons when travel is most active and rates for airfare and hotels are at their highest. Traveling during peak seasons will cost you more money. However; this will be further explained during the planning stage in Chapter Five.

- When traveling either domestically or internationally, always research affordable airline carriers that typically offer better deals. These airline companies may offer extra low fares when travelers fly certain days of the week. In the United States (U.S.), Spirit Airlines is known for their affordable flight fares. I have flown round-trip to Atlanta, Georgia, from Miami, Florida, for a mere twenty-five dollars. I have also flown round-trip to Washington, D.C., for eighty dollars. Sometimes Spirit airlines offer fares as low as nine dollars each way, not including taxes and fees. With fares this low, people on any budget can afford to travel.

In Europe, EasyJet is an affordable airline carrier in which anyone can purchase cheap flights. EasyJet flies across Europe from Great Britain to Spain, from Spain to Switzerland, and from Switzerland to Morocco. Since EasyJet is a European-based airline, all prices are listed in euros. However, when purchasing a flight, the purchaser is able to convert the total amount of the final charges into their native currency without incurring any additional charges. When I vacationed in Europe, I flew on EasyJet from Paris, France, to Barcelona, Spain, for only fifty-nine dollars. By finding such low fares, I was able to visit multiple cities in Europe.

Asia Air is Asia's affordable airline carrier and offers prices throughout Asia starting from eighteen dollars. The common factor among these airlines is their ability to offer lower fares, which allows their customers the freedom to fly. Even though these fares are lower, customers are responsible for paying for extras, such as baggage fees, seat preference fees, onboard snacks, and drinks. However, even with these optional extra costs, these airline tickets can still be extremely affordable.

• When you book hotel and airfare combinations with travel agencies, brokers, or even travel Websites, you may receive a discount. Travel Websites such as Cheapcaribbean. com or Expedia.com offer vacation packages, inclusive of airfare and hotels at discounted rates. Whenever possible, I always book combination deals to save money.

• When possible, purchase travel excursions abroad. This way, you can attempt to negotiate the price and customize your travel tour. Every city I have vacationed in had their own recommended traveling companies, and it has been my experience that all are willing to negotiate the price. Customizing your tour can be very important, especially if your time for exploring is limited. Sometimes you can even negotiate the price of a hired driver who can offer you a private, more intimate tour.

• Traveling in groups is always a savvy thing to do. Many companies, especially excursion companies, offer discounts for group activities. Groups can always negotiate traveling expenses, such as taxis, hotel accommodations, and eateries. Being in a group reduces expenses by splitting costs and also ensures maximum safety while being in a foreign land.

• Research companies like Travelzoo,

Groupon, and Livingsocial for travel deals. These companies are global Internet companies that offer a selection of deals from getaways, events and activities, entertainment, to local deals. These deals are inclusive of international and domestic travel that includes discounted airfare, hotel stays, bed-and-breakfast stays, lodges, retreats, discounted tours, meals, car rentals, and so much more. Memberships for these global companies are free. The only requirement is an active e-mail address to receive daily and weekly updates.

- When traveling abroad, always know the foreign exchange rate of the country you are visiting. The exchange rate is the price of a nation's currency in the terms of another currency. It has two components: the domestic, which is the base currency, and the foreign, which is the counter currency. For example, US$1=0.75 euro, so the base currency will be the $1 and counter currency will be 0.75 Euro. The foreign exchange rate changes daily and oftentimes locations other than the airport offer lesser conversion fees. There are several Websites that offer foreign exchange currency rates such as xe.com. When planning any international trip, always check the exchange rate. Doing so can save a savvy traveler money in the process.

• If you plan to travel abroad, first determine how you will contact your loved ones back home. Do not go on vacation without having some way to contact your family or friends via the Internet, telephone, or Webcam. It is strongly recommended that you contact someone to inform them of your whereabouts and let them know how you are doing.

• While abroad, there are many ways you will be able to communicate with your family and friends. Before leaving on your trip, contact your cell phone company and inform them that you will be traveling internationally. By doing this, your cell phone company will be able to unlock your cell phone, so while traveling you will be able to make international calls. This will come at a price, however. Cell phone companies will charge a roaming fee which maybe based on your destination country. In Dubai, it cost me $4.95 per minute to make international calls; in South Africa, it only cost me $1.95 per minute. The only way to know how much your cell phone carrier will charge will be to contact them and ask or check their Website.

- Other options include purchasing prepaid calling cards, purchasing an international SIM card, using the telephone at your hotel, or the Internet. When purchasing calling cards, make sure they are international calling cards. If not, you will not be able to use them while traveling. I can recall when I went on a cruise with my loved ones. I purchased a regular calling card, thinking I would be able to use it anywhere. However, I quickly learned that it could only be used in the States. Since it was not an international calling card, it wouldn't work overseas. International calling cards can be purchased in your native country or abroad. Just make sure you purchase the correct one.

- If you choose to use the telephone at your hotel, you will be subjecting yourself to whatever cost the hotel charges, which can really add up. I wouldn't recommend this option except in extreme emergencies. Hotels are able to charge whatever they want; there is no minimum or maximum.

- With certain cell phones, you might be able to purchase international SIM cards that you can place in your cell phone and not incur roaming charges. However, you will have to determine if your cell phone is capable of this. With the Internet, there are other options, such as Skype, Tango, WhatsApp messenger, or using your e-mail. Both Skype and Tango are software applications that allow users to make voice calls over the Internet. If the person you are calling has the application downloaded on their telephone or computer, then Skype and/or Tango is FREE. If the person does not have a Skype or Tango account, then you would need to purchase credits on your cell phone to make international calls. However, in order to make any calls via Skype or Tango, regardless if you purchased credits or not, you must first be connected to the Internet to place a call.

• WhatsApp messenger is very similar to Skype and Tango in that it requires access to the Internet as well. WhatsApp is a FREE messaging application for smartphones that allows users to send images, audio messages, and video messages without having to pay for SMS. All of these applications must be downloaded on your cell phone, and they will help reduce the cost of traveling since they are offered for FREE.

CHAPTER 4

The Savvy Traveler Dos and Don'ts

WHILE TRAVELING, I have made numerous mistakes, which have led me to create a list of what I call the Dos and Don'ts of traveling. These Dos and Don'ts will help you to avoid the same mistakes I made when I first began my journeys. Some of my Dos and Don'ts may seem like common sense, however, it wasn't until I had a few unpleasant experiences that I vowed never to make the same mistakes again. Following are my 15 Dos and Don'ts of traveling.

1. Do not compromise safety to save money. It's okay to look for bargains but safety should always be your first priority. Find a safe place within a reputable area. To obtain information about safety, you can e-mail or call the hotel and/or the police department and request an

updated status of their criminal statistics.

I can recall on a prior trip to Johannesburg, South Africa, where my friend and I attempted to save money on hotel costs and stayed in an inconvenient location and a location which we did not know was unsafe. We chose the location because it was near some of the historical sites we were interested in sightseeing. However, when we arrived at the hotel, the hotel employees advised us that it was not safe to explore the town on our own regardless of the time of day. To overcome this hurdle, we decided to hire a private transportation company and take taxis to get around.

In the beginning, what we thought was a really good deal turned out to be a nightmare. Not only was it not safe for us to come and go as we pleased, we ended up spending more money than expected because we had to pay for transportation wherever we went. After this experience, I decided to never compromise my safety to save money again.

2. Do inform your family and friends that you will be traveling and let them know where you will be going. You should never travel abroad without photocopying your passport and leaving the copy with someone you trust. You

never know what could happen to your passport while on your trip. It's a possibility that you may lose your passport or it can be stolen. If you are an American citizen and your passport is lost or stolen, you should contact the U.S. Embassy or consulate in the country you are visiting immediately and obtain a replacement passport.

It is also a good idea to leave a copy of your itinerary with someone back home. Making your whereabouts known is important in the event someone needs to contact you. Do not allow unforeseen circumstances that may occur on a trip hinder you from enjoying yourself. Always be prepared. Remember, taking precautions is not being negative or thinking the worst; it's simply being a savvy traveler.

3. Do check the weather of your travel destination in advance. Do not assume the weather where you reside is the same worldwide. When checking the weather, keep in mind that the temperature in every country feels different. There is a clear distinction between seventy-five degrees in London as compared to seventy-five degrees in South Florida, so be sure to pack appropriately. Nothing is worse than packing a bunch of clothes and not being able to wear them because it is either too cold or too hot.

Think about it this way. If you do not pack accordingly, you will either have to purchase clothes to accommodate the weather or you can wear what you have. But wearing what you have could cause you to be too cold or too hot, which could lead to you becoming sick while on your vacation, and no one wants to potentially ruin a vacation for that reason. A savvy traveler is always properly prepared for any weather conditions, which includes packing a collapsible umbrella just in case it rains.

I can recall the first time I went to France. My family and I decided to go late spring before the peak tourist season. Unfortunately, I did not check the temperature in France before packing my luggage. That was a huge mistake. I received a rude awakening once I stepped off the plane. It was freezing outside. The temperature was in the low 50s, but the clothing I packed was for temperatures in the high 80s and 90s. I made the mistake of assuming the temperature in France would be the same as the temperature in my home state. Before I could begin to relax and enjoy my vacation, I had to go shopping for clothing that was more suitable for France's weather, causing me to spend money that was intended for my trip and forcing me to go over my intended budget.

4. Do check the U.S. Food and Drug Administration before traveling. Be sure to not consume any foods or ingredients that may be considered unsafe. I would recommend you pack daily vitamins and any other medications you might need just in case you fall ill while traveling. Prior to departing for South Africa, my doctor prescribed all types of medications; one included azithromycin, which is commonly used to treat or prevent certain bacterial infections. This drug was not a requirement for my trip, but my doctor thought it would be wise for me to have just in case I became sick from something I ate while there. Taking precautionary measures will always help reduce or eliminate unforeseen situations.

5. Do pack spare clothing in your carry-on bag just in case the airline loses your luggage and/ or you would like to freshen up in between connecting flights. A dress for women and a shirt and pair of pants or shorts for men would be sufficient as you want clothing that isn't too heavy and can easily be toted in your carry-on bag. Wearing comfortable clothing while traveling is a must, and wearing layers is a great idea to easily adjust to temperature changes. I would also recommend you include toiletries such as a toothbrush, toothpaste, mouthwash, and facial wash in your carry-on bag as well.

Keep in mind many international airports offer shower facilities for transit passengers free of charge and different airline companies offer sky clubs or lounges that includes showers, complimentary cocktails, food, and Wi-Fi. Membership to these clubs or lounges can be purchased or earned through frequent flyer programs.

6. Do check in for your flight ahead of time. This will allow you to choose your seating preference so you can be as comfortable as possible while flying. Using online tools are highly recommended to determine the seat that works best for you. Seat guru.com offers seat maps of aircraft commonly used by the most popular airline carriers. This Website offers in-depth information regarding the pitch and width of all available seats, as well as the number of seats on the aircraft. Before making your seat selection, you are able to read past flyer reviews, view traveler photos, as well as a color-coded seat map key. Also, checking into your flight ahead of time will give you the opportunity to upgrade your seat. If available, many airline carriers will offer reduced prices to upgrade your seat class at check-in.

7. Do bring something to read or to listen to, or anything that will occupy your time while

traveling. Remember, while on a flight, you are unable to move around freely as you please. You have very limited space and are only able to stand up during certain times during the flight. While many international flights include individual televisions located on the back of the headrest of the chair in front of you, some domestic flights do not. Some may only have one television every few rows located on the ceiling of the aircraft. With this option, you are unable to choose what station you would like to watch because it is chosen for you.

On the flights where each person has their own television set, you are given a selection of movies, music, and television shows you can watch. Some will be free of charge while others will be for a price. Thus, I would recommend bringing any portable entertainment you may have that is not too heavy or large in size and can easily be transported. Such items include portable televisions, laptops, iPads or iPods, books, and magazines. When I travel, I always bring a book to read, my iPod, and my tablet. Having something to occupy my time is essential to helping time pass while taking any flight, especially long international flights.

8. Do practice safety once abroad. Please

remember you are in a foreign land and the natives will know you are a tourist. If you are traveling with a group, make sure you all stay together as a group or if the group decides to separate, no one should venture off alone. Do practice a buddy system so someone is always accountable for the other. As previously mentioned, safety should always be your first priority. Just in case something was to occur, it is always better to be in a group as compared to being alone.

9. Do obey all the laws of the land when abroad. Do not assume that because you are not a citizen of the visiting country that their laws do not apply to you or that your country's laws will take precedence. Like the saying goes, "When in Rome, do as the Romans do." When I visited Dubai, in the United Arab Emirates, I found out there is a courtesy dress code. It is recommended that you adhere to the dress code to respect the culture of that land. Now, even though the dress code is a courtesy in certain places, it is mandatory in others. I also learned that many Middle Eastern countries have curfew rules, rules about unmarried couples sharing the same hotel room, and scheduled days that women and children, excluding men, can do certain activities.

In Dubai, there are some beaches that women and children can only visit on Mondays and men are not allowed at that time. Breaking any of the laws in Dubai could result in severe punishment, and I was not interested in finding out what type of punishment they provide. This is why it is important to research the country where you will be traveling instead of assuming that every place is the same.

10. Do research the culture of your destination country. If you are from the West, do not assume every country's culture is the same as yours or that your culture is superior. There are many online search engines, books, or travel guides that would provide you this information. For example, the left hand is considered unclean in India as it is used to perform matters associated with going to the restroom. Therefore, you should avoid using your left hand when coming in contact with food, touching people, passing or receiving objects from people, or giving money.

In Thailand, it is frowned upon to show public affection such as kissing and hugging and being confrontational or losing your temper in public. These behaviors are considered rude and can potentially bring dishonor to a person's family. Knowing a country's culture shows a sign of respect and will help to prevent any offense from occurring.

11. Do plan activities before going on your trip. Do not wait until you get there and decide what you would like to do. Doing so will only take away valuable time from your trip. Now if you are spontaneous, you don't have to worry about planning your activities. But if you are a planner, I would recommend having an itinerary. I do not recommend that every single hour is prearranged, but it is a good idea to have a tentative schedule with room for flexibility. You always want to have spare time while on vacation in case you receive a suggestion that you want to pursue or if you become interested in something else during your exploration.

My first time in Puerto Rico, I was so excited about going that I didn't even consider what I might do once I got there. Neither my friend nor I planned any activities. We thought we would merely see what the island had to offer and just go with the flow. We later found out that was a bad idea. Once we arrived at our hotel, we encountered some room issues that took awhile to settle. After all issues were settled, we went to the hotel's concierge desk to see what they would recommend, but unfortunately, the concierge's desk was closed for the day. So we took excursion flyers and decided to book activities the following morning.

When we attempted to book our excursions the following day, we were sadly informed that many of the activities we were interested in were sold out. Our two alternatives were to either forget about the activities that really caught our attention or to find our own transportation to the excursion sites. We considered taking taxis but found out that option would have been too expensive and public transportation was not recommended because all roads and signs were written in Spanish and neither my friend nor I spoke Spanish. So we rented a vehicle with a (GPS) and ventured out on our own. I'm sure you can imagine some of the difficulties we encountered when the GPS couldn't find a location and we attempted to communicate with the natives not knowing the language.

In the end, we did our best and made the most of our trip. Even though we were there for four days and three nights, we wasted an entire day trying to figure out where we wanted to go and how we were going to get there. If we would have properly planned, we could have avoided wasting an entire day and had more time to enjoy the island.

12. Do create a daily spending budget for your trip. Do not spend any money without having a budget. It's very easy to overspend. So make your budget as realistic as possible and stick to it.

   For instance, you decide to go on a three-day trip and take five hundred dollars in spending money. If you divide five hundred equally over the three days, you will have a daily budget of about one hundred sixty-five dollars per day. That may sound like a lot to some but while on vacation, the bills can quickly add up. For instance, taxis or other forms of transportation might cost fifty dollars and breakfast and lunch could be another fifty. If you're not paying attention, you could end up spending seventy-five dollars or more at dinner. That's when the lightbulb goes off. You're ten dollars over budget. This realization is actually a good thing. If you'd never created a budget you might run out of cash or have to overspend. But now you can adjust your spending and have enough money to enjoy the rest of your trip.

   If possible, I would always recommend at least one hundred dollars spending money per day for both domestic and international trips. One hundred dollars is usually enough to cover your meals, snacks, and sometimes even transportation costs. However, consider booking a hotel that offers free breakfasts. This gives you the option of saving on this meal expense and leaves you with extra cash for other expenses.

In addition, I would recommend that you purchase your excursions ahead of time so they don't come out of your daily traveling budget. However, if you are unable to do so, you can follow the example above and determine the maximum amount you would like to spend and stick to that.

Remember, vacationing is a luxury. While you do not need it to survive, you never want to run out of money while on vacation. A savvy traveler would never overspend while on vacation because once it's over, he or she may have incurred a new debt.

13. Do know the travel requirements. Have a printed airline itinerary on hand while traveling. This is a requirement to gain entry into certain countries, case in point, China. Also, know the luggage requirements of your selected airline carrier. Many airline companies charge a fee for checked bags for domestic flights and one free checked bag for international flights. Most airline companies allow

passengers one free personal item such as a handbag or a laptop bag and a carry-on bag regardless of domestic or international travels. However, all bags have to be a certain size and always remember to never overpack. Doing so will cost you money and a savvy traveler shouldn't overpay. Many times when traveling, we tend to overpack and bring unnecessary items that we don't need or use. We tend to carry around extra weight at an extra cost. Packing light means bringing only what you need. Anything else should stay at home.

Depending upon the status of your frequent flyer accounts, you may be able to have your baggage fees waived. When traveling to Honduras, I was able to have my checked baggage fees waived because of my frequent flyer or medallion status. I saved over one hundred and fifty dollars.

When traveling to South Africa, I wasn't as lucky. I hadn't made medallion status to have my baggage fees waived so I encountered the problem of over-the-limit luggage. The airline attendant informed me that I could reduce the weight in my checked bag or pay the hundred dollar over-the-limit fee. I decided to layer my clothing and place items in my carry-on bag to prevent from having to pay this fee.

For twenty-two hours I was struck walking around overdressed and with a heavy carry-on bag. By the end of my trip, I realized many of the items I packed I didn't even use. Items I would recommend you pack to avoid encountering this include: your daily hygiene products, toiletries, medications, a pair of comfortable walking shoes for sightseeing, a pair of shoes for the evening, comfortable clothing, and one or two dressy outfits just in case you would like to explore a night out on the town. Pack swimwear if you intend to go to the beach and appropriate coats for whatever weather you may encounter while on your trip.

14. Do mark the outside of your luggage with a nametag or an object that makes your bag easily identifiable, such as tying a string, ribbon, or bandana around the handle. Frequently while traveling you may come in contact with luggage that looks exactly like yours but is not. No one wants the luxury of having to return the wrong luggage to the airport after their initial departure. By personalizing your luggage, you will avoid this from happening and, in essence, save you time when looking for your luggage.

Do not have all your personal information in your suitcase, such as your Social Security card and/or birth certificate. You don't want to carry this information in your checked-through luggage just in case it is lost or stolen. If these items are needed for traveling purposes, always carry them with you.

15. Do make a habit of developing relationships while traveling which will make your traveling experience much more memorable and allow your vacation to go a lot smoother. One relationship I would highly recommend you develop is with the concierge at your hotel. Your concierge is available to answer any questions you might have about the hotel, offer suggestions about excursions, nightlife activities, make restaurant and spa reservations, and arrange transportation if or when needed. The concierge is there to guide you in the direction of your choice. I would still recommend you research different tourist attractions and activities you would like to do in advance and have an idea of what you would like to experience while on your trip.

My most memorable experience with a hotel's concierge was at the Westin in Cape Town, South Africa. I had just checked into my hotel and was ready to experience the night scene. I went to the concierge's desk and met a man by the name of Dan. He recommended that I head to Long Street. Long Street is made up of restaurants that offer traditional African dishes, international cuisine, arts and crafts, live Jazz music, karaoke, and nightclubs/bars where you can grab a bite to eat and dance the night away. Dan was extremely friendly and helpful and gave me his contact information at the hotel if I needed any assistance while I was out. He arranged round-trip taxi service to and from my hotel.

Once on Long Street, I was amazed. It was exactly what Dan had described. I located a karaoke bar that served food and was also the hot spot on a Wednesday night. That night I was introduced to some authentic South African food. By the end of the night, I was exhausted and ready to head back to the hotel. The next morning when I saw Dan and he asked me about my night, he told me he had been waiting on my call the night before because he wanted to make sure I got back to the hotel safely. He informed me that he made it his personal duty to ensure that every guest he assisted returned safely to the hotel. At the moment, I felt as if Dan was my guardian angel. Every time I saw him, he always offered a pleasant smile, asked me questions about my trip, offered suggestions on where I should go and what I should see next, and reminded me that he was there if I ever needed him.

CHAPTER 5

Planning: 'Tis the Season

NOW THAT I have shared my TIPS and Dos and Don'ts of traveling, next I will introduce to you my three-stage traveling process: the Planning, Execution, and Outcome (PEO) process for traveling. This three-stage traveling process will show you how to create a successful plan and execute your dream vacation while saving money during the process. During the planning stage, you will understand the importance of knowing where to travel, when to travel, and where to stay while traveling. The first and second steps to this stage teach you the importance of determining your destination and the time frame of your travels.

During the planning stage, it is imperative for you to do your research. As previously learned, to save money, it is always better to travel during the off-season as compared to the peak season. Hotel prices and airline fares are typically cheaper. Some hotels may even offer discounted or free meals, free attraction tickets, or tickets to local events if you stay during their off-season. However, during the off-season you may have to endure unpleasant weather conditions, such as cold temperatures and/or rainy weather.

These weather conditions may last a few hours or even a few days during your trip. You must determine if the possibility of unfavorable weather conditions outweigh the additional costs of traveling during peak seasons. Just remember, traveling during the off-season is usually less crowded than the peak season. This is extremely important if you are interested in doing a lot of major tourist attractions, which are typically busy during peak seasons.

I can recall that on my trip to England, my family and I decided to travel during the off-season to save money. Our flight alone saved us nearly four hundred dollars per person. Once in England, we found the weather to be unfavorable but bearable. It was cold but not freezing. In order to go out at night, we had to wear jackets or sweaters to stay warm, and even during the daytime, we had to wear long-sleeved shirts as the weather was pretty chilly. However, we did not allow the cold weather to interrupt our trip.

We were determined to have a good time, and we did. We saw all the major tourist attractions, including the Tower of London, the London Eye, Big Ben, and the Buckingham Palace. We even had time to visit the famous Ice Bar London, where everything from the walls, tables, bar top, and our personal drinking glasses were made out of ICE. Since the inside temperature was a negative five degrees Celsius, we were given thermal gloves and a jacket that had to be worn at all times while inside. This experience in itself was the highlight of my trip.

In the reverse scenario, my family and I decided to travel to Belize during their peak season. As previously noted, traveling during the peak season will incur additional costs, especially for airfare and hotel accommodations. Therefore, you must determine if the possibility of favorable weather conditions outweighs the additional costs of traveling during peak seasons. Our reasoning for choosing to vacation in Belize was their beaches. The best time to visit the beach would be during their summer months which happen to be their peak. Even though our airfare and hotel prices were higher traveling during their peak season as compared to their off-season, the experience we had was well worth the extra cost.

During our vacation, the weather was absolutely beautiful. There was little to no rain, many sunny days, and nice blue skies. The streets were crowded with tourists, but that was to be expected, especially since it was their peak season. While in Belize, my family and I were able to lounge in the sun and tour the city's major attractions. We had the opportunity to go horseback riding on the beach, hike the rain forest, and kayak in the coral reef. We were able to do everything we planned and had one of the best trips of our lives.

When deciding where you would like to visit, never forget the beauty and adventures within your own native country. Residing in the U.S. gives you easy access to many states that offer breathtaking views of monumental sites like the Grand Canyon in Arizona, the World War II Valor in the Pacific located in Hawaii, the Statue of Liberty in New York City,

Yellowstone National Park located in Montana, Idaho, and Wyoming, and the White House located in the District of Columbia. Since the economic downturn, many people have decided to limit their travel abroad, and instead, stay within the comforts of their own home or city, cleverly known as a "staycation." Still others pack their bags and go on weekend getaways to hotels or bed-and-breakfasts located near beaches, wine countries, or in mountainous states.

These trips can sometimes be more rewarding than traveling to another country because they will give you an opportunity to explore the natural splendor of your native homeland. The states of the U.S. are very diverse. All fifty states are unique and inviting in their own way. Being from a tropical state, I take pleasure in occasionally renting a hotel room on the beach and pretending to be a tourist in my own town. However, being from a tropical state means I am limited to my climate experiences. Therefore, I can also take pleasure in traveling to other states to embrace different climate changes from snow in Colorado to the desert in Arizona.

The first time I observed snow was at the age of twenty-six. My friend was working in Denver, Colorado, and invited me to join her for the weekend. She had previously earned hotel rewards points and had enough to redeem for our weekend stay in Denver. I had previously earned rewards points on my rewards credit card in which I had more than enough to redeem for a round-trip airline ticket free of charge. Thus, my first experience with snow cost me absolutely nothing for my flight and hotel accommodations.

Since neither one of us had ever been skiing, we

decided it would be a great idea to go skiing for the weekend. I rented a car and we drove to the ski resort, which was about two hours away. When we got to the resort, we were able to checkin and obtain our ski gear. Trying to ski was definitely a challenge for me. Grasping the concept of skiing while using ski lifts took me awhile to accomplish. I fell down so many times during the process that my behind was killing me, but in the end, I was happy I welcomed the opportunity to have a new experience, and now I can say I have skied.

After skiing, I decided to be a kid again and wanted to snow tube. Lucky for me, there was a snow tube site near the ski resort. Snow tubing was extremely fun. There were different slopes where I was able to race down at fast speeds on an inflated tube. I was also able to play in the snow, create a snow angel, and have my first snowball fight.

CHAPTER **6**

Planning: Planes, Trains, and Automobiles

NOW THAT YOU have determined where you would like to travel, the next step is to determine your method of travel. There are many routes to viewing the world, from backpacking, guided tours, to cruising and road trips. Each option is different and caters to the needs of the individual.

What is backpacking and who backpacks? Backpacking is an inexpensive way to travel that allows you to travel at your leisure. Anyone can backpack, but it is typically popular among young adults. Backpackers often pack light and normally travel with a backpack or light luggage that can easily be toted for any trip or for an extended period of time. Since packing is limited, backpackers only pack what they absolutely need, depending on where they will be traveling.

Backpackers will pack clothing suitable for

versatile weather, personal hygiene products, food, and water. Since backpacking is an economical form of traveling, a backpacker often looks for ways to reduce traveling costs by using public transportation, staying at motels or hostels, or with friends. They search for free or discounted tourist attractions and enjoy easy on the pocket meals from street vendors or local restaurants. They typically live like the locals while on their trips.

Backpackers don't just travel within the U.S.; they explore the world. Backpackers love to sightsee. Africa, Antarctica, Asia, Australia, Europe, Central and South America; all seven continents offer adventurous activities that every backpacker would love. From outdoor activities like hiking and mountain climbing to water activities like kayaking and water rafting, each destination is unique. Generally, this method of travel offers freedom to explore nature's beauty and experience the wilderness without having restraints on time and offers the opportunity to see the world while conserving money.

If you are interested in traveling, but you are not interested in the planning that comes with it, or you do not have the time to plan your dream vacation, then taking a guided tour may work best for you. Guided tours typically include your airfare, hotel accommodations, ground transportation, and some meals. Guided tours have a preset itinerary, which informs you of your daily activities as well as hotel selections in advance.

The conveniences of these tours are a major advantage since everything is planned for you. The only things you will have to do are pay for your trip, pack your luggage, and enjoy. The second convenience of a guided tour is being able to visit multiple cities in a short span of time. This is a great perk because it will ensure that you are able to visit each city's major attractions within a limited time frame. The third convenience of a guided tour is that every hour of your day is not preplanned. You will be given free time for independent activities usually in the late afternoon, evening, or at night. This is a perfect way for you to venture off on your own (with a buddy, if possible), hang with the locals, do some shopping, or just stay at your hotel and relax.

The last major convenience to using a guided tour is ensuring you will have a tour staff that will be able to communicate with you in your native tongue. This is something that is extremely important to me because I have visited many countries where English was not their first language. Trying to find someone who was able to communicate with me felt like a mission at times. However, when using a guided tour, communication problems will be the least of your worries. There will be a tour guide who will be willing to assist you and someone you will be able to communicate with and make your travels an easier transition.

The only major disadvantage of a guided tour is the cost. Guided tours tend to be more expensive than backpacking, independent travels, and do-it-yourself tours. Before discounting this option because of money, I would recommend you analyze the above conveniences and determine if they outweigh the additional costs for choosing a guided tour.

Cruising is a great way to experience multiple vacation destinations on one trip. Cruise lines like

Carnival, Norwegian, and Royal Caribbean offer many itineraries, which include far-off destinations from the Caribbean to the Mediterranean, from the coast of Australia to the coast of Asia. Cruising allows you to sit back and view the world from the top of a multilevel ship or from the comfort of your balcony suite.

Cruising works great for family vacations since the price of any cruise is inclusive of your room, meals, coffee and teas, and onboard activities. Prices, however, do not include soft drinks, alcoholic beverages, spa treatments, or offshore excursions. With that said, cruising is still great for every budget. The cost for your cruise will depend on the stateroom you select and the number of guests sharing your stateroom.

Depending upon your ship, each stateroom can occupy a minimum of one guest with a maximum of four or five guests. There are typically four stateroom types on every cruise ship and each type varies by size. The least expensive rooms are the interior rooms. Interior rooms are the smallest rooms on any ship. These rooms are basic rooms that include twin beds, bunk beds, or a queen-sized bed, are generally located at various levels on the ship, and usually do not have access to sunlight; for example, a porthole or window.

The ocean-view staterooms feature a picture window or a porthole that usually has two twin beds or a queen-sized bed. Ocean-view staterooms offer a little more space for comfort and relaxation than the interior rooms. The balcony stateroom includes a furnished balcony, which offers excellent views of the seas and ports from the privacy of your room. These rooms usually include refrigerators, minibars, and spacious closets. This kind of room is great for relaxing and people watching and offers outside access to the ocean air.

Lastly, suites are the largest staterooms on any ship. These rooms typically include a separate sitting area, a sofa bed, a whirlpool bathtub, as well as a fully furnished balcony. Suites are also the most expensive staterooms. In my opinion, cruising is fun because it is extremely affordable for every traveler's budget, from the eco-friendly traveler who is interested in saving money, to the traveler who appreciates luxury and doesn't mind spending extra money for the additional amenities.

While cruising you will never have to worry about what you should do when aboard the ship because there are many prescheduled activities for every age group divided into morning, afternoon, and evening sessions. Such activities include morning stretching or aerobic classes, afternoon towel folding classes and dance competitions, and evening comedy and games shows.

Cruises even offer activities for the youth. Youth activities are typically classified into different age groups. Age groups can start as early as two years old and extend to preteen. Youth activities are supervised by adult counselors, and it's the counselors' job to ensure the youngsters are safe and having a good time. With so much going on each cruise, it's very easy for anyone to become indecisive about the next activity he or she should do.

In addition, many of the onboard activities vary per cruise ship, especially if you are embarking on a theme cruise. Theme cruises are cruises with enhanced onboard experiences. Theme cruises come in all forms with itineraries including: music, dance, food and wine, sports, photography, TV and film, as well as arts and crafts, faith-based, gaming, technology, and history and world affairs.

There are theme cruises available to fit the interests of almost every individual. An advantage of a theme cruise is bringing together individuals who share similar curiosities. Quite possibly, you may receive a more enriching vacation experience, learn something new about your interest, and network, all while having a great time.

Theme cruises are offered by various cruise lines, and itineraries may vary per year. Theme cruises also have a daily preset schedule of activities just like a regular cruise in which guests can choose to participate. Regardless of whether you're interested in a regular or theme cruise, cruising is an affordable and excellent method of traveling and viewing the world.

I enjoy saving money, and my favorite method for exploring the world allows me to do just that. For my twenty-eighth birthday, I went to an all-inclusive resort in Cancun, Mexico. This was my first time having the all-inclusive experience, and I absolutely loved it. Even though the price was a little more than just purchasing a regular vacation package, the extra benefits definitely outweighed the additional initial costs.

All-inclusive typically cover meals, alcoholic and nonalcoholic beverages, entertainment such as nightly shows, cooking classes, and water activities which can include snorkeling and/or wind surfing, and even gratuities. The hotel I stayed in while in Cancun was inclusive of meals that included twenty-four hour in-room dining, minibar service, signature liquor brands in bars, restaurants, access to the media center with computers and printers, and wireless Internet access. It was well equipped with everything I wanted or needed so I never had to leave the resort.

The staff catered to my every need and whim, whether in-room, at bars, lounging on the beach, or at the pool. They were there to assist and answer any questions I had. When I first arrived at my hotel, the staff was superaccommodating. They went above and beyond to ensure that my transition from the hotel entrance into my room was hassle-and worry-free.

Everywhere in the hotel the staff greeted me by name and asked about my stay. When I was interested in booking tours or excursions, all I had to do was contact the front desk, provide my credit card information, the date and time of the excursions, and everything was prearranged. The only thing I had to do was meet the tour company in the front of the lobby on the day of the excursion and have fun. The extra attention and superb customer service I received was worth the additional costs I incurred for selecting the all-inclusive option.

Just as there are theme cruises that cater to the specific needs and desires of their guests, there are all-inclusive resorts that cater to the specific needs and desires of their guests. Such accommodations include adults-only and couples-only resorts, meaning no children are allowed. The minimum age requirement varies per location but generally the minimum age requirement is 18 to check into either of these accommodations.

Both adults- and couples-only resorts are mostly located in the Caribbean: Antigua, Aruba, the Bahamas, Dominican Republic, Jamaica, Mexico, and St. Lucia. The adults-only accommodations typically offer a luxurious and peaceful environment in which guests are able to pamper themselves by day and become socialites by night. The couples-only resorts are for lovebirds who would like to indulge in romance by having intimate accommodations and restaurants, access to some of the world's most exotic beaches, extravagant amenities, and concierge services. The couples-only resorts also offer a one-on-one relaxation service in which guests may be assigned personalized staff to assist them when needed. Both provide a relaxing and upscale vacation where adults can getaway and enjoy their retreat.

Connecting flights are also an avenue for viewing the world. Many people are pessimistic about connecting flights. They never want a delay in reaching their final destination. However, when traveling to certain destinations, especially those far away, a connecting flight may be your only option. Yes, nonstop flights are more desirable, but they can be rather pricey.

If you are willing to choose a connecting flight, you may be able to save a few hundred dollars that could be used toward your hotel and/or excursions. Connecting flights can also allow you the opportunity to experience another city during your layover. For instance, if you have a layover for five or more hours, you could be adventurous, catch a taxi, and take a whirlwind tour of the city or meet up with an old friend for a nice meal.

If you really want to be creative, you could book the first leg of your flight of your trip for day one and your connecting flight the following day. Either way, you could turn your connecting flight into an optimistic experience and have the opportunity to view another city or country during the process. How wonderful would it be to explore a new city without having to purchase an extra plane ticket to do so? You might even discover that you truly enjoyed your added trip and decide to go back another time for a longer period.

Connecting flights also give you the option of resting in between flights. This might be extremely helpful if you are someone who experiences really bad jet lag or motion sickness. The con of choosing your connecting flight to view the world include: incurring additional costs. For example, when you decide to venture outside the airport during your layover, anything you decide to do will cost money. If you decide to book your connecting flight for the following day and stay in your connecting location overnight, you will incur an additional cost of finding a place to sleep. However, as you now know, you will discover there is an easy solution to this as there are affordable places you can stay such as hostels or motels. Choosing to view the world via connecting flights is a very doable means of traveling, especially if you have determined your budget and figured out a way to make it work.

The epiphany of venturing out to the layover city came to me during my travels to and from South Africa. My entire flight was about twenty-two hours upon departing, including one connecting flight, and twenty-four hours returning, including two connecting flights. The actual flight time was between eighteen to twenty hours each way. As I was departing the U.S. for South Africa, I was so excited about traveling to the beautiful country that I really didn't care about the traveling time or my connecting flight. I could have cared less about my layover because I only had one connecting flight.

Upon returning home, it finally struck me that I had *three* flights ahead of me. The first leg of my trip was my flight from Cape Town, South Africa, to Amsterdam, The Netherlands. This flight was about eleven-and-a-half hours. The second leg of my trip was from Amsterdam to New York City, New York, and this flight was about nine hours. My final flight departed from New York City for Miami, Florida. This flight was about three hours. After the first leg of my trip was completed, I was extremely exhausted, my legs were hurting, and my body felt cramped. I had a three-hour layover in Amsterdam and during those three hours, I dreaded the fact that my upcoming flight was going to be for another nine hours. So I considered changing my flight to the following morning, however, the price was too expensive. So I came to terms with it and got on my original flight back home. In total, it took me over twenty-four hours to reach home. I told myself that I would never make that mistake again. If I ever had multiple connecting flights or an extended layover after a long flight in the future, I would try to book my connecting flight for the following day.

On my very next trip, I decided todo just that. My flight from the U.S. to Rome, Italy, had a connecting flight with a six-hour layover in Barcelona, Spain. I booked the second leg of my flight the following day after my initial departure.

The flight from the U.S. to Barcelona was only six hours, but I decided to spend the day there and depart in the morning for Rome. Since I was only in Barcelona for the night, I decided to stay at a very inexpensive hotel in an area called Las Ramblas, which is a central location in Barcelona that is popular among both tourists and locals. This area is full of shopping, eateries, and nightlife. I remembered researching the best and safest location to stay. I asked friends and coworkers, read reviews on different travel-related sites, and e-mailed the hotel in which I was interested to obtain information before I decided to book.

Once I arrived at my hotel, I was satisfied with my choice. It was in a highly desirable location, clean, and had the level of safety I required. While in Barcelona, I sampled authentic Spanish food like paella and croquettes, hung with the locals, and completed a city tour which allowed me to see Barcelona's beautiful architecture, including the Barcelona Cathedral and Gothic Quarter, the world-famous Picasso museum, and sandy beaches all on the back of a moped. This one-day retreat excited me so much, that whenever the opportunity presents, I always book my connecting flights the following day, or if I have a five- or more hour layover in flight, I turn my otherwise idle time into minitrips.

Over the years, I have been very successful at viewing many cities and countries by choosing connecting flights, whether it was a connecting flight a day after my original departure or an extended layover. When I traveled to Tokyo, Japan, I had the option to select a connecting flight with a layover in San Francisco, California. The layover time ranged from one to five hours without incurring any additional charges.

I was excited about visiting San Francisco since I heard it was a very beautiful city. With my five-hour layover, I had just enough time to complete a one-and-a-half hour city tour and head back to the airport to catch my next flight to Tokyo. To minimize my costs, I caught the public train downtown to the location of my tour. The one-and-a-half hour tour allowed me to see some of San Francisco's historic landmarks from Pier 39 to the Golden Gate Bridge. While on tour, I wasn't pressed for time. I was able to even stop at a souvenir shop to purchase a shot glass for my collection. I take pride in my minitrips and enjoy showing others how to capitalize on their traveling experiences.

As we have previously learned, airfare can be really expensive, especially if you do not purchase your airline ticket in advance. For those of you who may have a fear of flying or just enjoy the ability to travel at your leisure, I would recommend road trips. Road trips can be really pleasurable as you are able to create your own itinerary, make frequent stops while en route, and enjoy the scenery along your journey. When taking a road trip, I would always recommend bringing a map or a global positioning system (GPS) to direct you along your drive, some entertainment that will help you pass time, such as music or books, and someone or something to keep you company. I would also recommend bringing light snacks and something to drink when driving long distances.

Road trips can fit any budget and are also good

for family trips. For those who can afford RVs, they might be a really good investment because they are like vacation homes on wheels. For those of you who cannot, you have the option of renting a vehicle or driving your own car. But if you drive your own car, the only expense you will incur is gas and/or tolls. If you choose to drive your vehicle, before your trip, I would suggest you have a scheduled routine maintenance completed on your car to ensure that it will be safe for the distance you will be driving. If you decide to bring others along, everyone can share these expenses. So whether you rent a vehicle or drive, your vehicle is totally up to you. Remember, a savvy traveler is always looking for ways to reduce expenses without compromising safety.

Depending on where you would like to go, road trips can last a few hours, or even days. My first road trip was to New Orleans, Louisiana, for the 15th Annual Essence Festival. New Orleans is approximately twelve hours from my hometown. A group of friends and I were interested in going, however, the cost for our airfare was outside of our budgets. We decided to embark on a road trip that would reduce the overall costs of our trip and allow us to have additional monies once we arrived in New Orleans. We decided to drive one of our vehicles as another method for reducing costs since we all had fairly new and well-maintained cars.

Since we were able to save money by not purchasing airline tickets, we were able to spend a little extra on our hotel. We researched and located a reasonably priced higher-end hotel across from the Ernest N. Morial Convention Center, which was an essential location because it was where many of the events for the festival were held that year. Our hotel did require us to pay for hotel parking, but even totaling the amount we paid for gas, highway tolls, and hotel parking, it was a lot less than purchasing our plane tickets.

While in New Orleans, we found it was easier to take public transportation compared to driving to get around town. Getting stuck in traffic and having to pay additional fees for parking would have just added unnecessary stress to our trip. Our road trip turned out to have a pleasurable ending because my friends and I not only enjoyed the festival, we had a blast on our journey too. Better yet, we saved money during the process.

CHAPTER 7

Planning: Passports, Visas, and Immunizations

EVERYTHING YOU HAVE learned thus far has been great information. However, you won't be able to leave your native country without the proper documentation; a passport book or a passport card. A passport book allows you to travel internationally by airplane, car, bus, train, and cruise. A passport card allows international travel by land and sea only. Passport cards are valid for travel to and from Canada, Mexico, the Caribbean, and Bermuda at land border crossings and seaports-of-entry. Taking international cruises are possible with a passport card, however, the cruise would have to leave from a seaport within the U.S. and return back to a seaport within the U.S.

There are many similarities between the passport book and passport card, for example, their duration of validity and the processing time to obtain them. Both are valid for about ten years for adults and five years for minors under age sixteen, and the processing time can take up to four weeks.

The differences between the passport book and passport card include the size and cost. A passport book is about 5″ x 3.5″ in size, and a passport card is about the size of a wallet-sized driver's license. The cost for first-time applicants for the passport book is about one hundred thirty-five dollars for adults and one hundred five dollars for children under age sixteen, whereas the cost of a passport card is about fifty-five dollars for adults and forty dollars for children under age sixteen.

Your traveling style and budget will determine what you will need. I personally know individuals who have a fear of flying and have vowed to never step foot on an airplane, and some of them have not been on an airplane in over fifty years. These individuals have made up their minds that flying is not for them but have not allowed their fear to prevent them from doing the very thing they love, which is to travel. Instead, they take cruises and road trips regularly. For these individuals, a passport card would work best for them.

Now that we have learned about the difference between passport books and passport cards, when traveling internationally, remember to do your research and determine if your destination country requires a visa for entrance. Keep in mind, U.S. citizens do not need a U.S. visa to travel but may need a visa issued by the country they are visiting. A visa is a document that authorizes a person to enter or leave the country for which it is issued. If you are unsure if the country you are visiting requires one, or do not know where to look, visit travel.state.gov. This Website offers a variety of information, such as the forms to fill out, time frame of completion, and costs of visas. There are different restrictions for visas for business visitors or tourists, study abroad programs, and workers in different countries.

A relative of mine planned a trip to Beijing, China. She was superexcited and ready to learn in-depth about the Chinese culture and visit the major tourist attractions, including the Great Wall of China. She flew over twenty hours and once she arrived at customs in China, she was in for a rude awakening. She was denied entry into China because she had not applied for and received a valid visa issued by the Chinese Embassy to enter their country. No matter how much she cried and pleaded, the Chinese officials denied her entry. Since she was already in Asia, she decided to detour and go to another country where a visa was not required. By doing so, she incurred additional expenses from having to alter her plane ticket and book new hotels. She also lost money on prepurchased excursions. That day she learned a valuable lesson: you must do your research before planning and taking any trip.

Depending on the country you visit, an international visa may not be required if you are only visiting that country for a short period of time. When I traveled from Tokyo, Japan, to Hong Kong, I had a connecting flight in Shanghai, China. Since I had never been to China, I chose a connecting flight with the longest layover that afforded me twenty hours to tour Shanghai. When researching if a visa was required to enter Shanghai, I found out that one was not required as long as I was in the country for less than seventy-two hours. So I was able to visit Shanghai, complete another "minitrip," obtain an extra stamp on my passport, and add to my souvenir collection without needing an international visa. Now that's the example of a savvy traveler.

Besides having a visa, immunizations may also be required and/or recommended to enter your destination country. The difference between a required and recommended vaccination is the traveler must have and maybe asked to show proof that he or she received the required vaccination before gaining entrance into the visiting country. Required vaccinations are to ensure the safety of the traveler as well as the safety of the people with whom the traveler may come in contact while visiting. A recommended vaccination is not mandatory for the traveler to receive or show proof to gain entry into the visiting country, but only a recommendation to take precautionary measures. It will be up to the traveler to decide whether to get the recommended vaccination.

The first time I received vaccinations was for my trip to South Africa. I researched what vaccinations I needed and discovered I had to have Hepatitis A, Hepatitis B, Typhoid, and Influenza vaccinations, as well as a prescription for malaria pills before I could embark on my journey. At first I was terrified about receiving the vaccinations because I hate needles, but in order for me to depart for my dream vacation, I knew I had to have them and decided to get them done as soon as possible to get them out of the way. I was told by my doctor I needed to have all vaccinations completed at least four to six weeks prior to my departure so my immune system could build up a tolerance to the vaccinations.

Once I knew what vaccinations I needed, my next step was to find a location to have them completed. I located a few travel clinics in my area. After giving them a call, I found out that vaccinations were pricey and the price of each vaccination varied. I also found out that some travel clinics did not accept health insurance and/or some health insurance companies do not reimburse for every vaccination. I would highly recommend that you contact your health insurance carrier before going to have your vaccinations completed to see if your particular insurance plan provides reimbursement or covers the costs of any of the needed vaccinations. If so, you could reduce your out-of-pocket expenses and save money on your vaccinations. Fortunately for me, my health insurance did cover three out of the five vaccinations I needed, so I only had to pay for two of them, thus saving me around three hundred dollars.

CHAPTER 8

The Planning Process: Places to Stay

DURING THE PLANNING stage, you decide where to travel, your method for travel, and where you should stay. There are a variety of places one can stay from hotels, motels, vacation homes, and hostels. The prices of hotels and motels can really add up depending on their ranking, customer reviews, and restaurant options.

Motels, at times, can be more affordable than hotels. However, as previously learned, when traveling during the off-season, hotels tend to offer rooms at a reduced rate. There are several differences between hotels and motels. Hotels are typically in high-rise buildings in prime locations, financial districts, and places where there are popular tourist attractions. Rooms tend to be larger in hotels as compared to motels, and motels are typically single story with fewer rooms than hotels. Many motels are located along interstate highways, and have exterior room entrances that resemble apartment-style living. Hotels offer considerably more amenities and services than motels such as Jacuzzis, saunas, gyms, and/or business centers.

There are also differences between boutique hotels and hotel chains. A boutique hotel is an individually owned and operated hotel that has fewer rooms than a hotel chain. They offer more of an intimate setting with full accommodations and sometimes are better priced than the hotel chain. Hotel chains can be located worldwide and are managed by various companies. There is a certain expectation that may come with a chain hotel, especially one known for luxury. Depending upon where you travel will determine if you have a preference. When choosing any of the above accommodations, it's recommended that you read reliable, recently dated reviews. Various online resources such as tripadvisor.com allow you to read and comment about your hotel experience.

Other places to consider include hostels and vacation home rentals. Hostels are very inexpensive and vary by size based on location. They provide suitable accommodations where guests can rent a bed, which usually is a bunk bed, and share a bathroom. Rooms can be co-ed or same sex; however, private rooms may be available for an additional fee.

Traditional hostels include dormitory-style accommodations while newer hostels can resemble hotel-style rooms and suites. Many people who are interested in backpacking prefer this option because they can simply rest for the night and are on their way in the morning. The cheapest I have paid for a hostel was fifteen dollars per night.

When trekking Madrid, I chose a hostel in the heart of the City Centre. The hostel was unisex but individual rooms were same sex. I was a little hesitant to try a hostel, but when I saw the price and knew I was only going to be in town for two days, I decided to give it a try. When I arrived at the multilevel building, the front entrance was decorated with beautiful flowers. Upon entering, there was a lounge that included a lobby, which was fully furnished with an entertainment theater and a bar. The lounge led to an elevator that went up seven floors. On each floor were several rooms with four or six beds in each and very few rooms were single occupancy. Each room was also equipped with private bathrooms. The only furniture in the bedrooms was the beds themselves and the bathrooms that came without toiletries. There were no televisions, cables boxes, VCRs, etc., so it was clear that the room was meant for sleeping and lounging only.

Vacation home rentals, bed-and-breakfasts (B&B), and time-shares are becoming very popular as people decide to travel in groups and with their families. Many vacation homes surround prime locations like beachfronts, downtown high-rises, major tourist attractions, and have easy access to public transportation. Vacation homes consist of apartments, cabins, villas, condos, townhomes, and houses. I would highly recommend a vacation home rental, as these are actual homes equipped with full kitchens which will allow every traveler to save on meals.

Vacation homes are larger than the average hotel room. When traveling, we all know that everyone wants and needs their personal space to relax and rejuvenate. Vacation homes also offer amenities just as a hotel and are very cost-effective. Every savvy traveler yearns to save money while traveling, and since the average cost for a vacation home per person can be less than the average cost of a hotel room per person, this arrangement will allow them to do just that.

The first time I stayed in a vacation home was on an island in the Bahamas. It was a beautiful and luxurious beachfront home facing the ocean. All rooms came with spectacular views of the beach, and the master bedroom had a balcony that opened to the calming, fresh air of the blue seas. It had five bedrooms and three-and-a-half bathrooms and included an entertainment/home theater room, game room, gourmet kitchen, and dining room, which was fully furnished with contemporary and sophisticated interior designs with HDTVs and Blu-Ray systems throughout the home. The open kitchen had all the amenities that included a dishwasher, refrigerator, and microwave. The outdoors included a hot tub with a waterfall leading to a private pool, direct access to the beach with beachside cabanas, and a mesmerizing garden with multiple hammocks for relaxing.

The vacation home came with a housekeeping and maid service that prepared meals, cleaned, and catered to our every need. This home was in a prime location so that rental vehicles were not needed. Everything was within walking distance from local restaurants, pubs, and shopping centers. Even while on the beach, we had easy access to a variety of water sports from parasailing, jet skiing, to windsurfing. Since our vacation home was plush, we enjoyed relaxing and lounging around while soaking in the beauty of our impeccable beachfront home.

As previously mentioned, bed-and-breakfasts (B&Bs) have risen in popularity among travelers. B&Bs are located worldwide and are typically private homes, which offer overnight accommodations that include breakfast and light snacks. Guests usually have their own private bedroom and bathroom and the owners of the private homes generally serve as the hosts and perform the cooking and cleaning. In some countries, B&Bs are classified into categories determined by the Ministry of Tourism. In others, the tourists are the ones who classify the B&Bs. Based on my experience, many B&Bs are more expensive than hostels. They may be nicely decorated with antique furniture to create a historical feel, have a more modern or traditional décor, and offer free wireless Internet, free parking, nightly entertainment, and nightly snacks. There are blogs and review Websites where past guests can state their opinion about the B&B, and other travelers can read their reviews and determine if a B&B is suitable for them.

Lastly, time-shares are another vacation option for places to stay. Time-shares are properties in which multiple parties have ownership and rights to that property. Each owner is allotted a time frame for their use of the time-share, and if an owner chooses not to use their allotted time, they may elect to lease it.

Leasing a time-share can be a very affordable way of reducing traveling costs. Just as the vacation home can save money, so can a time-share. Time-shares are typically condominiums but can also be hotel rooms. A person choosing to lease their time-share may be willing to negotiate the price, especially if they know they will not be using their allotted time for that year. When traveling, no matter what housing option you choose, you will always save money as long as you research and plan in advance.

CHAPTER 9

Execution

THE SECOND STAGE of the Planning, Execution, and Outcome (PEO) process for traveling is execution. During this stage, you will learn how to turn your dream vacation into reality. After you have determined your destination, the next step is to execute and go. Before you pack your bags and jet off, there is one important thing you must do: determine how you will fund your trip.

The execution stage will teach you how to create a budget, the importance of sticking to that budget, and creatively finding ways to save money. Now, don't allow the word *budget* scare you. Creating a budget can be fun. Don't dread the mathematics portion of it; focus on completing another step that is bringing you one step closer to your vacation of a lifetime.

In creating your budget, determine a minimum and a maximum amount you would like to save just for traveling. Determine a realistic amount of money you would be able to set aside weekly, biweekly, monthly, or even bimonthly. If it becomes extremely difficult to add a traveling expense within your daily budget, another way to save money could be to use annual bonuses and/or any refund monies from annual income tax returns. These monies are a guarantee regardless of the amount, and they can be used to fund your vacation.

Before creating any budget, always remember . . Budgets are away for you to decide how you should spend your money. I would recommend that you calculate your monthly income after taxes because this will give you a true estimate of your total monthly earnings. Next, I would recommend you calculate your monthly expenses. In order to do this, you will have to save all your receipts for a couple of weeks or a month to determine your monthly spending habits.

Once you have an estimate of all of your expenses, separate them into two categories: "necessities" and "luxuries." Expenses which are "necessities" include mortgage or rent payments, utility bills, and groceries. Expenses which are "luxuries" include entertainment, dining out, and/or gifts. Some expenses could go into either category, such as grooming costs and clothing. When I am stuck determining the category of an expense, I ask myself this question: "Can I live without it?" If I can, then that expense is placed into the "luxury" category; if I cannot, it is placed into the "necessity" category.

Now that you have determined your monthly income and expenses and have categorized your expenses, the next step is to set a realistic goal of how much you would be able to save. By setting this goal, you will be able to measure if you were successful or not in your efforts. I would recommend that you look for ways to reduce your weekly or monthly spending, including reducing weekly entertainment and/or dining out. The extra monies saved can be used for your trip.

Being creative and finding ways to save money can help make the budgeting process much more pleasurable. Creative ways of saving money and reducing daily expenses include: carpooling, reducing coffee runs, limiting shopping sprees, and using coupons. Reducing the amount of your everyday bills include downsizing from a premier cable package to a basic cable package and choosing a lesser expensive Internet package. When creating a budget, it does not mean you cannot live nor does it mean you cannot have fun while saving money during the process.

I would recommend you research FREE activities your city offers, such as art shows, entrances into museums, city tours, going to the beach, or having picnics in the park. Always remember, once that budget has been set, it is nothing more than a budget until it is put into action. When I created my first traveling budget, I decided it was realistic for me to set aside fifty dollars biweekly. If at any time I was able to save more, I would, but fifty dollars biweekly would always be my minimum. Once I reached a certain amount in my traveling savings account, I was able to start paying for my trips.

The second phase of the execution process includes different payment methods for purchasing your trips. Once you achieve your saving goals and have all or a significant amount of the funds needed to finance your dream vacation, you are in a good place.

To top it off, you may not even have to pay for the entire trip up front. There are many companies that offer installment payment plans, where an initial deposit consists of a percentage of your trip and the final payment is required seven to eight weeks before the departure of your trip. Cruise lines are notorious for this. They allow you to make an initial deposit and pay the remaining balance before your departure date.

For my trip to Honduras, I used a travel-related Website and got a really great deal. I chose this site because it offered payment installments. I had to make an initial deposit of two hundred fifty dollars and the final payment was due six weeks prior to our departure, and if I wanted to, I could have made monthly payments and paid off my trip before the final payment was due. I have used companies that offer payment installments on my trips to Jamaica and South Africa. Since this has been a great experience for me, I would highly recommend using this option for everyone.

CHAPTER 10

Outcome

SO FAR, YOU have learned the importance of not only planning and executing your plans but how both processes can be extremely exciting and easy to do. The final stage in the Planning, Execution, and Outcome (PEO) process is, of course, outcome. This stage allows you to celebrate your hard work and the results of accomplishing your traveling goal.

Imagine all of the wonderful pictures and memories you will have, the experiences you will gain, the new friends you will meet, and the historical sites you will see, all because you decided to take the time out to plan and execute the trip you have always wanted to take. All of the budgeting, saving, and planning will have finally paid off. This chapter lists personal stories of my previous traveling experiences.

Las Vegas

I began planning my first major trip as early as eighteen years old. Ever since I could remember,

Las Vegas, Nevada, had always sparked my interest. The big-city lights, attractions, entertainment, and renowned chef dining were things I desired to experience. However, the minimum age requirement to really enjoy Las Vegas, Nevada, is twenty-one, so I knew I had a few years to wait. Once I turned twenty-one, I decided to begin planning and saving for my trip. I obtained part-time employment in addition to my primary employment and began saving an extra fifty dollars per pay period to ensure I would have more than enough money for my trip. By the time I was twenty-two, I was not only old enough to go to Las Vegas, my finances were in order as well. I had saved over twelve hundred dollars, which covered my round-trip airfare and hotel stay. I researched what experiences I would like to have and decided to purchase my attraction tickets once I arrived in Las Vegas. A few months after my birthday, I boarded my flight and was off to my destination.

Once I arrived in Las Vegas, I was amazed. The airport itself had the appearance of a casino located on the famous Las Vegas Strip. There were bright magical lights and slot machines everywhere. In addition, there were shops of all kinds and information attendants available to answer any questions about the city and to sell excursions. Once I exited the airport, the desert heat welcomed me. It was approximately one hundred degrees outside. There were also taxis, luxury cars, and limos waiting to escort guests to their hotels. Once I arrived at my hotel, I was astonished. There were palm trees, multiple casinos, lounges, spas, theaters, and museums—everything I could imagine was all conveniently located at my fingertips.

Even though I was only in Las Vegas for four days, I was able to accomplish a great deal. I had the chance to attend two pool/day parties, one at Wet Republic at the MGM Grand Hotel & Casino and the other at the Tao Beach pool party at the Venetian Resort Hotel & Casino. I also attended a Cirque du Soleil show; Mystère at Treasure Island Hotel, shopped at Caesar's Palace, rode the gondola at the Venetian Resort Hotel & Casino, took a bus tour to Hoover Dam, witnessed a water show at the Fountains of Bellagio Hotel, viewed Las Vegas from the Eiffel Tower at Paris Las Vegas Hotel and Casino, enjoyed the roller coaster at New York-New York Hotel and Casino and visited Egypt via the Luxor Casino Hotel. The only thing I would have changed was the time of year I decided to go. I had no idea how extremely hot it could get in the summertime in Las Vegas. Yet, despite the extremely gruesome heat, I still had an excellent trip. By planning in advance and taking on a second job to save money, the execution and outcome of my first major trip was a huge success.

Europe

Since I gained knowledge on what it takes to accomplish a successful trip, I decided to repeat the same process when planning my first international trip. I began saving money and working overtime to fund my trip. I created my budgets and began saving seventy-five dollars or more biweekly. It took me nearly two years to bring this dream into reality, but these two years were worth the wait. My family and friend decided we all wanted to experience Europe together, so the planning process was put in full effect.

We researched extensively the most visited countries in Europe, historical landmarks, the best and safest locations to stay, and the most recommended excursions and tours among tourists. We finally narrowed it down to the countries we were excited about seeing. We researched different tours and cruises, but none of them had the itinerary we sought. Originally, we wanted to begin our tour in London and end it in Italy. We later found out that unless we wanted to spend an entire month in Europe, we were in over our heads.

We located many tours that included all of our destinations, but we wouldn't have been able to stay in each country but for a day or two and, in our opinion, that would not provide us ample time to tour each city. We also found the same problem when looking at Mediterranean cruises. The Mediterranean cruises that caught our attention averaged a total of seven to twelve days with an average of eight countries, depending on the cruise lines. However, the average time in each port varied, and we found very few cruise lines that included overnight itineraries, and the cruises with overnight itineraries only had one per cruise.

After further research, we decided to be realistic about the amount of time we wanted to travel and what were the most important things we wanted to experience on our first international trip. In the end, we decided to tour England, France, Spain, and the Netherlands within two weeks. We divided our time in each location based on the activities of interest. We decided to spend four days and three nights in Paris and Barcelona because of the different vineyards, museums, and nightlife we wanted to experience, and three days and two nights in London and Amsterdam. Depending on what you want to do and see will determine how long you should visit a city, but remember, if you get there and do not experience everything you wanted to, you can always go back.

As soon as we knew where we wanted to go and for how long, we had to look for places to stay. We decided to stay downtown and around city centers. We found them to be very tourist-friendly with easy access to public transportation, such as trains and buses, and they offered a variety of food selections. Many of the activities we wanted to do were in these locations. All hotels we chose were three stars or above. On this trip, we learned that each country had their own classifications of what a three or higher star hotel or motel meant. Before deciding on hotels, we read hotel reviews on different Websites and compared what past guests were saying. In the end, all of the hotels we booked were based off of convenience, safety, location, and pricing to ensure we stayed within our budget.

Once our hotel accommodations were booked, we were able to research the different activities in each country. We knew that in France we had to go and see the *Mona Lisa* at the famous Grand Louvre museum. We knew when we went to Netherlands we had to go to the Van Gogh museum. We researched different tour Websites to determine which ones offered the best prices and if any companies offered discounts if more than one tour was purchased. We also found out that if we were affiliated with any membership organizations such as AAA, we might be able to obtain additional discounts on tours and excursions. While abroad, my traveling buddies and I had the experience of a lifetime. We had ample time to see and do everything we could imagine.

Facing Fear in Jamaica

During the short few years that I have traveled, I have learned a valuable lesson. The outcome of any of my trips was always in my control. If I wanted to have a fun, successful, and worry-free travel, then I needed to prepare and plan in advance. Sometimes, events beyond our control occur while traveling, for instance, bad weather, stolen items, or catastrophes. Since they are beyond our control, the only thing we can do is learn from them.

Fear, on the other hand, is within our control. Fear, in my opinion, is a hindrance and keeps us in hiding. Fear will stop you from living up to your true potential and allow you to miss out on life. Fear will stop you from traveling if you believe you cannot afford it. Fear will stop you from flying if you are afraid to get on an airplane, and fear will stop you from cruising if you are afraid of water. I used to allow fear to keep me in hiding. I was afraid of deep water as I had a fear of drowning. I had taken swimming lessons in the past but could not overcome my fear. I enjoyed going to the beaches, jet skiing, and parasailing, but while I was doing these things, fear was always with me. It was like it was following me everywhere I went and was a complete annoyance to me.

Recently, my friends and I planned a trip to Negril, Jamaica, and I was ecstatic as I had never been there. Everyone I was traveling with was talking about cliff diving at Rick's Café. I refused to be the only person who couldn't cliff dive because I didn't know how to swim. Before my departure to Negril, I attempted swimming lessons, but I wasn't able to overcome my fear before my travels. So I promised myself that I wouldn't take another trip without knowing how to swim. Upon my return, I started back with my swimming lessons, and it wasn't easy facing my fear. It was hard work, but in the end, I faced my fear head-on . . . and I won. Today, I am proud to say I can swim, and it was an exhilarating time to swim at Lantau Beach on my trip to Hong Kong.

Traveling has also taught me so much about myself. I have learned that the world in which we live is filled with differences. Traveling has exposed me to these differences and taught me to embrace them. By using the Planning, Execution, and Outcome process for traveling, you too can enhance your exposure and create traveling stories and lifelong memories.

Regardless of your chosen method of travel, I would highly encourage you to travel. Choosing to step out of your comfort zone and see the world is an amazing feeling in which words are hard to describe. Like awaking to a sunset at the top of Mt. Fuji after climbing the entire day before, drinking coconut water out of a fresh coconut while lounging on a beach in Barbados, and enjoying a live belly dance around a campfire under the stars in Abu Dhabi. These memories have made me a better person, and I know you will experience the same. Take lots of pictures and send me a postcard!

CPSIA information can be obtained at www.ICGtesting.com
Printed in the USA
LVOW11s0906010315

428809LV00001B/19/P